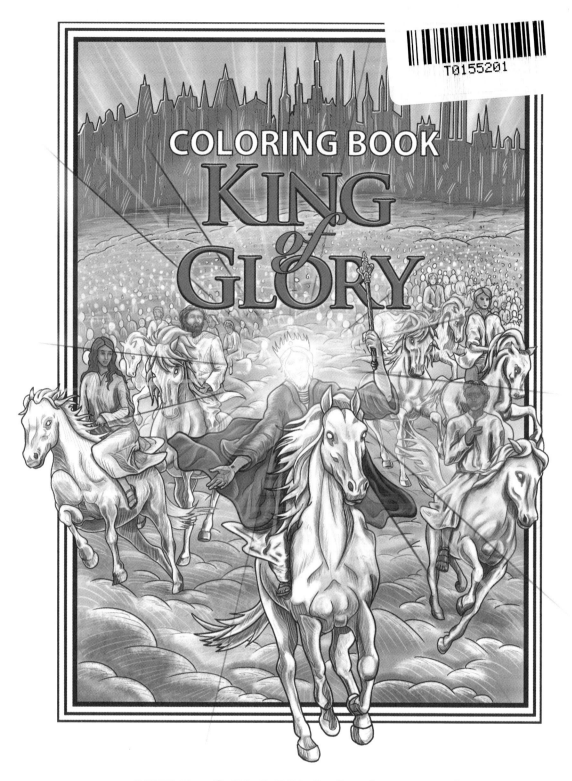

KING of GLORY Coloring Book

Coloring Book artwork by Cole Phail
adapted from KING of GLORY picture book
by author P. D. Bramsen and artist Arminda San Martín

Copyright © 2019 ROCK International
ISBN 978-1-62041-009-7
Printed in USA

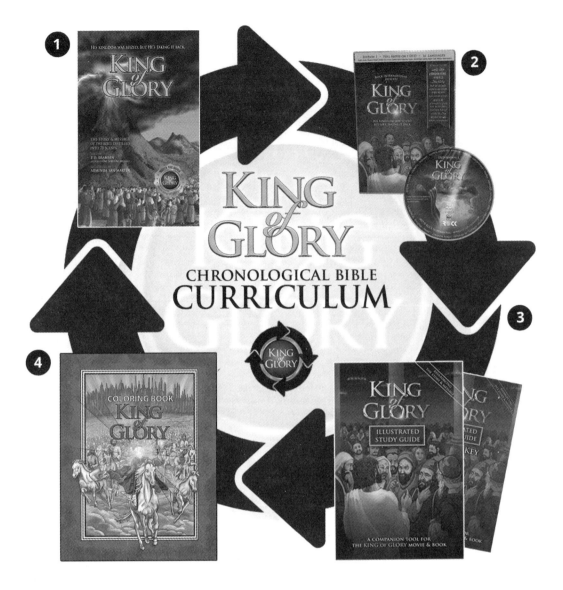

1 70-SCENE PICTURE BOOK
With plain yet profound text alongside 70 biblically-accurate paintings, this panoramic journey through the Scriptures tells God's story and message in a way that makes sense to people of all ages and cultures.

2 15-EPISODE MOVIE
This riveting word-for-word animation of the book unfolds the big picture of the Bible in a way kids can really grasp. For adults, it gives a framework for understanding the Scriptures from Genesis to Revelation.

3 15-LESSON STUDY GUIDE & ANSWER KEY
Filled with stunning illustrations from the book and movie, the information, questions and exercises in this workbook reinforce the foundational truths embedded in the KING of GLORY movie and book.

4 70-SCENE COLORING BOOK
These thought-provoking coloring pictures provide a meaningful activity to go with the movie and book and help cement God's chronological story and message into the minds of all who color them.

www.king-of-glory.com • resources@rockintl.org • 1-208-719-9312
Deep discounts for case quantities

1

3

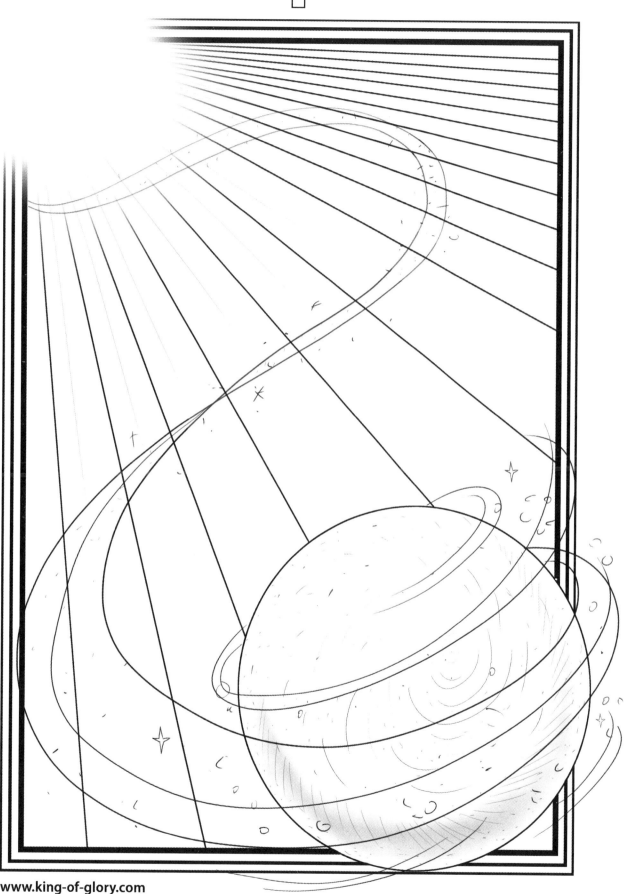

7

9

11

13

21

23

25

32

38

43

61

62

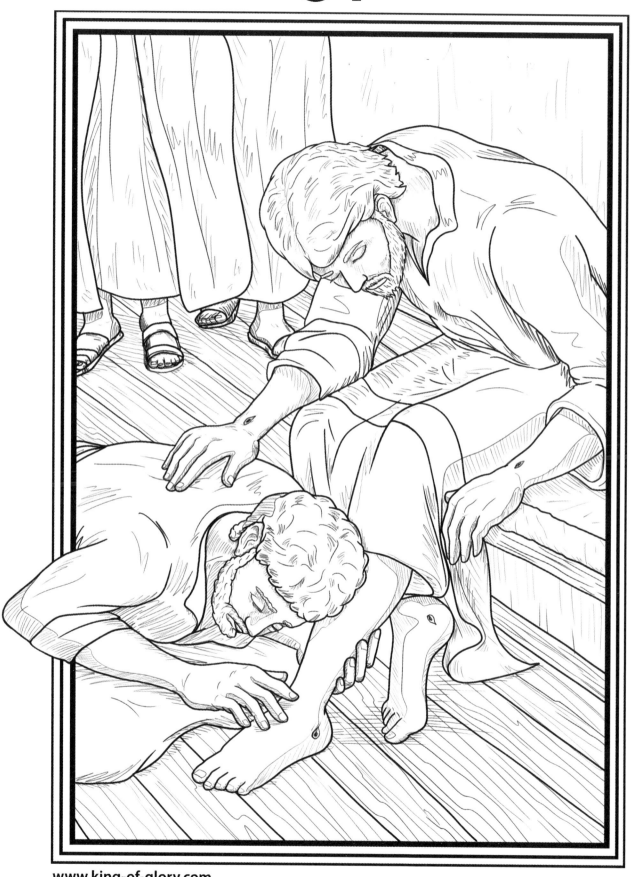